Student Loans Don't Have to Bite

Take the Mystery Out of Student Loans

StudentLoanInstructor.com

Student Loans Don't Have to Bite

Website: www.StudentLoanInstructor.com
Email: info@StudentLoanInstructor.com

Printed in the United States of America

ISBN: 9780985607012

Disclaimer

Due to the nature of the information being provided in this book, certain information is subject to change as federal law mandates. The federal government, specifically the U.S. Department of Education, can change loan interest rates, processes, programs, etc. at any time.

Student Loan Instructor is not responsible for any damages or loss of any form. When making academic and/or college financial aid decisions always consult with a college representative.

What is Federal Student Aid?

In the U.S., students wanting to earn a post-secondary education can apply for money to pay for college expenses. Under Title IV of the Higher Education Act of 1965, money is made available to college students through Federal Student Aid, an office of the U.S. Department of Education. This money is commonly called financial aid and hereafter this term will be used. Financial aid consists of grants, loans and work-study. **In this book we will be focusing on student loans.**

Tip: To better understand the federal student aid program, the process and the different types of aid available which includes grants, work study and student loans get our eBook, *"10 Simple Steps to College Financial Aid"*.

What Are Student Loans?

Student loans are funds (money) you can borrow to help pay for your post-secondary (college) education expenses. One main difference between student loans and other loans is that you can postpone (delay) repaying student loans until you have separated from school. **What does it mean to separate from school?** You separate from college by graduating, withdrawing, dropping out, or enrolling less than half time (usually less than 6 credits).

The student loans received from Federal Student Aid are commonly called **FEDERAL Direct Loans.**

Student Loans Consist of 3 Main Parts

- **Principal**: the actual dollar amount you borrow
- **Interest rate**: the cost you are charged for borrowing the money, stated as a percentage
- **Fees**: (commonly stated as loan or origination fee) usually the cost of processing the loan, stated in a percentage of the loan amount

Federal Student Aid offers several different types of student loans. See the different types of federal student loans below.

Types of Federal Direct Student Loans

Subsidized Federal Direct Stafford Loan: You must demonstrate financial need to receive a subsidized loan. The U.S. Dept of Education will pay (subsidize) the interest that accrues on this loan while enrolled at least half time and under other circumstances. The interest rates & fee for subsidized loans disbursed during July 1, 2011 to June 30, 2012 for undergraduates are 3.4% and for graduates 6.8%. There is an origination fee of 1% when the loan is disbursed.

Unsubsidized Federal Direct Stafford Loan: Financial need is not a requirement to obtain an unsubsidized loan. You are responsible for repaying the interest charge that accrues on your unsubsidized loan once the loan has been disbursed (paid). Your lender or loan servicer will send you a letter every quarter (every 3 months) indicating how much interest has accrued. You can choose to pay the interest while you are in school and during a period of deferment or forbearance. You can also choose to defer paying the interest charges until you start repaying the loan. However, this will cause your student loan debt to increase.

For military students, interest does not accrue while serving for up to 60 months. The interest rate for unsubsidized loans disbursed during July 1, 2011 to June 30, 2012 is 6.8% for undergraduate and graduate students. There is an origination fee of 1% when the loan is disbursed.

Parent Direct Plus Loan: This is a loan parents can obtain to help pay the cost of education for their dependent undergraduate children. The interest rate for this loan disbursed during July 1, 2011 to June 30, 2012 is 7.9% for undergraduate students. There is an origination fee of 4% when the loan is disbursed.

Graduate Direct Plus Loan: A loan graduate and professional degree seeking students may obtain to help pay for their own education up to the cost of attendance. The interest rate for this loan disbursed during July 1, 2011 to June 30, 2012 is 7.9% for graduates & professional degree borrowers. There is an origination fee of 4% when the loan is disbursed.

Federal Perkins Loan: This loan is funded through the U.S. Department of Education, a federal agency, and your college/university. Not all schools offer the Perkins Loan. Students can use this loan for their undergraduate & graduate degree programs. Additionally, it is offered to students who demonstrate financial need, are enrolled full-time or part-time & must be repaid to your school. The interest rate for this loan disbursed during July 1, 2011 to June 30, 2012 is 5% fixed. There are no other fees associated with this loan.

Direct Consolidation Loan: This loan allows students and parent borrowers to combine multiple federal education loans into one loan with one monthly payment. There is no credit check or income verification needed for approval.

Note: You cannot combine or consolidate the Parent Plus loan your parents borrowed for you with your student loans. The interest rate for this loan is the weighted average of the interest rates of all the federal loans you consolidate, the rate will never exceed 8.25%

*The interest rates listed above are for loans disbursed July 1, 2011 to June 30, 2012. Go to the Federal Student Aid website, www.studentaid.ed.gov to find the interest rates for future periods.

What about Student Loans Offered by Banks & Other Financial Institutions?

Students can also borrow money for college through financial institutions such as banks and credit unions. However, these educational loans are considered **private or alternative** student loans. Private/alternative loans are NOT federal student loans. There is a big difference between private and federal student loans so make sure you have a solid understanding of both.

There are **two advantages to borrowing private or alternative student loans**. First, most private student loans can cover up to 100% of the cost of attendance (COA). Second, you do not need to complete the Free Application for Federal Student Aid (FAFSA) to receive a private loan.

There are also **many disadvantages to borrowing private or alternative student loans** which include:

- Loan application is **subject to a credit check** and the results will determine your interest rate
- Interest rate is variable, meaning it can go up or down, throughout the life of the loan. Whereas, federal student loan interest rates are fixed for the life of the loan
- May not have deferment or forbearance option. This means if you are unable to pay your loans at some point, you may not have the option to postpone your payments
- May need a co-signor to qualify for the student loan
- Federal repayment plans, student loan forgiveness and assistance programs do not apply to private/alternative student loans

Tip: Avoid borrowing private/alternative student loans as much as possible. The bottom line is you should always apply for and use all the Federal Direct Student Loans you are eligible for first before considering private/alternative student loans.

Federal Direct Student Loans are a better deal for the following reasons:

- Backed by the U.S. Department of Education
- Multiple repayment plans
- Longer repayment periods
- Interest rates are fixed over the life of the loan
- No credit check or co-signor needed
- Many programs available to help repay, forgive or cancel some or all of your federal student loan debt
- Deferment & forbearance options available to temporarily postpone payments if you experience financial hardship during repayment

Minimizing Your Need of Student Loans

There are many steps you can take to minimize the amount of student loans you borrow. Some of these ideas will require sacrifice of free time and a disciplined lifestyle during your years in college.

1. **Consider starting your first two years of college at a community college**. Tuition at a community college is significantly less expensive than four year colleges. Attending the first two years at a community college will allow you to earn your associates degree and then transfer as a junior into a four year institution to complete your bachelor's degree. Taking this route will save you money because you will borrow fewer loans, if any, to pay for your education expenses.

2. **Consider your state colleges**. By attending your state college or university you can pay in-state tuition which can be considerably lower than the cost of an out of state, Ivy League or private school. Also, beware of for pro-fit or online schools. They can be very costly as well.

3. **Consider working at your college/university to possibly get free tuition assistance**. Check your college job website or department postings for part-time positions. The types of jobs you can find include tutoring, library assistants, computer lab assistants, etc. Colleges/universities often offer employees a specified number of free college credits per semester or academic year.

4. **Check if your college offers a tuition payment plan**. If you work while attending college, paying your college expenses may be easier with a payment plan. These payment plans are usually setup as monthly installments with little or no fees and interest.

5. **Research for scholarships and apply early**. Scholarships eligibility can be based on different criteria such as academic, athletic, specific program of study, religious affiliations, etc. Some students may wonder if it is worth applying for scholarships. The answer is yes! Be willing to put in the time to search and apply for scholarships early.

   Visit fastweb.com or collegeaid.com to search and apply for scholarships.

Be careful of scholarship scams. You will find many organizations offering scholarship information for a fee, especially online. The main goal of these scholarship scams is to steal your identity and/or money.

How do you know if you are being sold fictitious scholarship information? Look for the red flags below.

- The company does not provide contact information such as a working phone number and address.
- You are told no other company provides the information and/or access to scholarships.
- You are guaranteed that you are going to get a scholarship. No company can really guarantee you are going to qualify for a scholarship because eligibility is based on many factors.
- You are asked for personal information such as social security number, date of birth, bank/credit card account, etc. Never release such information to anyone or company unless you are absolutely sure of what you are getting involved in.
- You are asked to pay a fee to get a scholarship or your money back. You should **never** have to pay to get a scholarship. **This is the biggest red flag.**

Check out the Federal Trade Commission website to learn more about scholarship scams at www.ftc.gov/scholarshipscams.

6. **Utilize your employer tuition assistance program.**
   If you work for a company check with the human resource department to see if they offer tuition assistance. Keep in mind some may offer to pay the cost of the tuition up front.

You must show proof of enrollment by completing a form or providing a copy of your class schedule. Your company may also decide to reimburse you after successfully completing your course(s). Most companies require you earn a grade of C or better in your courses to receive tuition reimbursement.

Check for military education benefits. The U.S. armed forces which include soldiers, airmen, sailors, guardsmen, marines, reservists and veterans will pay for you to get a college education. The military offers tuition assistance, credit for service and scholarships. The key is to know what is available, what you qualify for and using the benefits before they expire. One website that has been very informative on military education benefits is military.com

Note: Your spouse and dependents may also qualify for military education assistance.

There are two popular military education benefits, the Montgomery GI Bill and Post 9/11 GI Bill. Both education benefits are administered by the Department of Veterans Affairs. The GI Bill has several programs that help active duty, Guard and Reserve service members, veterans and their families earn postsecondary degrees, certification, vocational training or attend career school.

Depending on your status, you can get up to 100% of your education & living expenses covered...all tax free.

Other programs include the Veterans Educational Assistance Program (VEAP) and the Survivors' & Dependents' Educational program (DEA). Visit the Department of Veterans Affairs website; www.va.gov to learn more and apply.

Take action now and apply for all benefits available to you if you are considering going or returning to college. Keep in mind, you may qualify for more than one education benefit at a time so take time to research, ask questions and apply.

We will now discuss how to apply for and repay federal student loans.

Applying for Federal Student Loans

You would apply for federal student loans the same way you apply for other federal student aid; by completing the Free Application for Federal Student Aid (FAFSA). The only way you will know what you actually qualify for is by completing the FAFSA. Do not call your school's financial aid office and ask for an estimate. The determination is not made at the school level but at the federal level by Federal Student Aid.

The key is to start the process early enough to allow you enough time to plan and budget for school.

The FAFSA is administered by Federal Student Aid, an office of the U.S. Department of Education, which is a federal agency. Any questions you may have about the application while filling it out should be directed to this office. They are helpful and conveniently available by phone, email and web chat. Look for their contact information at www.fafsa.ed.gov

To receive the Federal Direct Loans you are eligible for

- You must be accepted for admission at a college or university
- You must be enrolled in an eligible program of study. Check with your school's financial aid office to determine if your program of choice qualifies for financial aid. Usually, you cannot receive federal student aid for enrichment courses or continuing education units.
- You must be enrolled in classes at least half time.
- Sign your Master Promissory Note (MPN)
- Complete the Entrance Counseling tutorial

A **Master Promissory Note** is a document you sign promising to repay (payback) the student loans you borrow even if you do not complete your education, are not satisfied or do not like the education you receive or even if you are unemployed. If you have the same lender for all of your student loans you may need to complete only one master promissory note.

The **Entrance Counseling tutorial** must be completed by first time borrowers of federal student loans. It can be completed online or in person at your college financial aid office. The Entrance Counseling tutorial provides useful information about ways to prepare to effectively repay your loans. Some of the tips provided include how to create a budget, understanding key financial aid terms, etc.

Repaying Your Student Loans

After separating from school, if you accepted federal student loans, you are entitled to a grace period before you start repaying your student loans. If you borrowed private student loans, you may not have a grace period after separating from school. This is one of the disadvantages of borrowing private student loans.

Types of Federal Student Loans	Repayment Begins
Subsidized Federal Direct Stafford Loan	6 months after separating from school or your enrollment drops to less than half time
Unsubsidized Federal Direct Stafford Loan	6 months after separating from school or your enrollment drops to less than half time
Federal Perkins Loan	9 months after separating from school or your enrollment drops to less than half time
Direct PLUS Loan	No grace period, repayment begins 60 days after the loan has disbursed (paid), can defer payment while enrolled at least half time in school

Exit Counseling: Before leaving, your college financial aid office will contact you to go through an exit counseling tutorial. It is similar to the entrance counseling, but the focus is on your rights and responsibilities as a borrower.

Grace period: During your grace period, you will be contacted by the loan servicer or lender with information on how much your payments will be, due date and where and how to make your payments.

Tip: As long as you are enrolled half time in an eligible program, you can defer (postpone) making payments toward your federal student loans. For example, if you complete your bachelor degree program and will enroll in classes within 6 months into a graduate program, you must notify your loan servicer that you are continuing your education and request a deferment.

Note: If you decide to continue your education you must **request a deferment** from your lender or loan servicer to temporarily postpone payments. This is very important. Many students ruin their credit by defaulting on their student loans simply because they failed to communicate with their lender or loan servicer in a timely manner. If you already started making payments, continue to do so until you receive approval of your deferment. Keep in mind the longer you postpone paying your student loans the more interest you will accrue and have to pay back.

Tip: If you are a parent considering the Direct Plus loan for your child please give it serious thought before doing so.

First, repayment starts while your child is still in school. Second, if your child chooses to withdraw or quit school, you are still responsible for the loan. Lastly, the loan is in your name only not your child's so the burden of repayment falls on you.

Where Do You Send Your Student Loan Payments?

Your lender or loan servicer is responsible for billing and receipt of your **federal** student loan payments NOT your school. However, if you have a **Perkins Loan**, you need to make your payments to the school where you borrowed the loan.

What is a loan servicer? Lenders will often hire a company to perform the billing functions for its loans. This company is called a loan servicer. Before July 1, 2010, you were able to go to most banks or other financial institutions like Sallie Mae® to request a **federal** student loan under the Federal Family Education Loan (FFEL) program.

This is no longer an option. The banks and financial institutions were middleman. They have been eliminated in the federal student loan process with the passing of the SAFRA Act, which was part of the Health Care & Education Reconciliation Act. Starting July 1, 2010, all federal Stafford, Direct PLUS & Consolidation loans will be administered by Direct Loans. Thus, the lender for any federal student loans you received on or after July 1, 2010 will be Direct Loans.

Note: Direct Loans may use different loan servicers, such as Great Lakes Education Loan Services, to manage the billing of your student loans. So your federal student loan bills may come from a loan servicer. If you are unsure who is sending you your student loan bills, contact Direct Loans at (800) 848-0979 to confirm.

**Private or alternative student loans on the other hand usually are paid to the lender which can be a bank, credit union or other financial institution.

Important: The loan borrowers often forget about which often cause them to go into default is the Perkins Loan. Perkins Loans are provided by both the federal government and your school. However, repayment must be made to the school. Students often forget to contact their school to make payment arrangements, request deferment or forbearance. Our book, *"10 Simple Steps to College Financial Aid"* explains more about this loan.

Keep your contact information current: If you move or change your phone number, make sure your lender or loan servicer is informed. You want to make sure you receive all loan communications in a timely manner.

Always contact your lender and explain your situation. Don't ignore your responsibility toward your student loans. They will work with you. There are multiple repayment options available.

What Interest Will You Be Paying?

The interest rate for your federal student loans is determined by federal law. Federal Direct Loans have fixed interest rates and will remain the same throughout the life of the loan. For example, if you borrowed a subsidized loan during award year 2011-2012 and the interest rate you were charge is 3.4%, that interest rate will remain the same for the life of that loan.

Now if you borrow an additional subsidize loan during award year 2012-2013 your interest rate may be higher or lower than 3.4% however whatever it is, it will remain the same for the entire life of that loan as well.

Note: If you have private/alternative student loans, your interest rate is most likely variable. If the interest rate is variable, that means the rate can go up or down at any time during the life of the loan. You can determine the type of interest rate you have by reviewing your loan documents or by contacting your lender or loan servicer.

Tip: Sign up for email and bill notifications from your lender's or loan servicer website. Doing so is beneficial for the following reasons:

- Quicker access to loan information
- Convenient way to make loan payments
- Decrease your risk of identity theft

How to Make Payments Toward Your Student Loans?

The best way to make payments toward your student loan debt is by signing up for automatic bank draft. This means you will have your payments electronically pulled from your bank account on a certain day each month. Many lenders offer a discount on the interest rate if you sign up for electronic debit. Direct Loans offers a discount of .25% off your interest rate when you sign up for electronic debit. The less interest you have to pay the faster you can pay off your student loans.

If your payment due date is not convenient, contact your lender or loan servicer in order for it to be changed. Rent or mortgage payments are usually due at the beginning of each month which can consume a substantial portion of your paycheck. If this is your situation, schedule your due date a few days after the second or third paycheck of each month to ensure you always have the funds in your account.

Tip: Sign up for direct deposit with your employer so your paycheck can be directly deposited into your bank account. This will help you make timely payments on your debts and expenses.

You may also pay through the lender or loan servicer website. Usually you can pay with a credit card or bank account. You can also pay by mailing a check each month. Contact your lender to ensure you have the correct mailing address for payments. When paying by check, keep in mind that mail processing times vary. If payment is not received by the due date, late fees may be charged to your account. For this reason, paying your bills by mail is not recommended.

What Are the Different Repayment Plans Available for Federal Student Loans?

An overview of the different repayment plans offered by Direct Loans is listed below. For more details on any of the repayment plans go to www.studentaid.ed.gov.

Standard Repayment: This plan allows you to pay a fixed amount each month until the loan is paid in full. Your monthly payments will be at least $50. You have 10 years to pay the loan off under the standard repayment plan. You pay the least amount of interest under this repayment plan.

Extended Repayment: To qualify for this plan, you must have more than $30,000 in student loans held by Direct Loans. You have 25 years for repayment with two payment options. **(1)** fixed payments, where you pay the same amount each month **(2)** graduated payments – you will start paying a lower monthly payment and then every two years the monthly payment will increase.

The **graduated payments** are advantageous especially if you start your career making less money. As you start making more money later in your career, you should be able to pay a bit more toward your student loans. Though this plan helps you make reasonable payments in the beginning, you will pay more interest throughout the life of the loan.

Graduated Repayment: The payments for this plan starts low and then increases every two years. You have 10 years to repay the loan under this plan. If you expect your income to increase over time, this is a good repayment plan to choose, especially if your current income is low. Your payment will never be less than the accrued interest between payments.

Income Contingent Repayment (ICR): Monthly payments are calculated each year base on your adjusted gross income (AGI). If you are married, your spouse's income is also included along with your family size and total Direct Loan balance. Under this plan, the maximum repayment period is 25 years. If you still have a balance, the unpaid balance will be discharged. This plan is not available for PLUS Loan borrowers.

Income Sensitive Repayment: This plan is similar to the income contingent repayment plan; however, it is targeted for students who borrowed federal Stafford loans under the Federal Family Education Loan (FFEL) Program. Starting July 1, 2010, the FFEL Program was eliminated with the passing of the SAFRA Act.

Income Base Repayment (IBR): This plan also takes your adjusted gross income into consideration and your family size. Basically, Direct Loans takes a certain percentage of the difference between your AGI and 150% of the poverty guideline set by the Department of Health & Human Services for your family and the state. You should consider this plan during any period you experience partial financial hardship. Your monthly student loan payments may be adjusted annually. Under this plan, the maximum repayment period is 25 years. If you still have a balance, the unpaid balance will be cancelled.

Tip: The IBR plan is the best plan if you are experiencing financial hardship. It is also one of the eligible repayment plans you can be on if you decide to pursue the Public Service Loan Forgiveness (PSLF) program. Under this plan your repayment period would be 10 years thereafter any remaining balance would be forgiven. You will learn more about the PSLF program later in this book.

Note: The regulations for these repayment plans are subject to change. To stay up to date with the latest changes of each repayment plan, visit Direct Loans periodically at www.direct.ed.gov

Let's now discuss how you can consolidate your federal student loans.

Consolidating Your Student Loans

Once you enter repayment you may find it difficult to make separate payments for each loan you accepted while in college. What can you do? First, consolidate all your federal student loans.

What exactly does it mean to consolidate your loans? Let's say you borrowed several subsidized, unsubsidized loans and Perkins loans during your years in college. Take all of these federal student loans & have them bundled into one loan. This process is called ***consolidation***. Consolidation allows you to take multiple federal student loans and combine them into a single loan. You can also add the student loans you borrowed from other schools you attended as long as they are federal student loans.

Example: You borrowed federal student loans from University of ABC during your freshman and sophomore year. You then transferred to University of LMN to complete your junior and senior year and borrowed additional student loans. Later, you borrowed more federal student loans when you studied at University XYZ for your graduate degree. Now you have completed your education and need to start repaying your student loans. You may get three different bills. This is what you do:

Step 1: Contact each of your lenders to get the exact amount of each type of student loan (subsidized, unsubsidized, Perkins and/or Graduate Direct PLUS) you borrowed.

Step 2: Go to the Direct Loan Servicing Center website, http://www.direct.ed.gov and complete the consolidation paperwork.

Step 3: Direct Loans will pay off all your federal student loans you have with other lenders. They will take the balance of all those loans they paid off and combine it into one big loan which will be called Direct Consolidation Loan. You may see the balances separated as subsidize and unsubsidized loans but you will only have to make one payment each month to Direct Loans.

If you borrowed federal student loans on or after July 2010, then your lender for your **federal** student loans will automatically be Direct Loans no matter what school you attended. So in this case, just contact Direct Loans and let them know that you want to consolidate the federal student loans you have with them. They will walk you through the process. The entire process usually takes about 30 to 45 days to complete. If they ask for verification of documents, quickly provide them.

Tip: Always ask if you can fax the documents to them. Follow up a day later to confirm they received it.

Tip: If you ever have to mail documents to your lender or loan servicer, use priority mail and pay the nominal fee for delivery confirmation. This will ensure your documents are received in a verifiable and timely manner.

Note: Unfortunately, you cannot consolidate private and federal loans together. They are like oil and water. All of your federal subsidized & unsubsidized Stafford Loans, Perkins Loan & Graduate Direct PLUS Loan can be combined. You **cannot** combine the PLUS Loan your parents borrowed for you with your own student loans.

What are the advantages of consolidating your federal student loans?

- You make one payment toward your federal student loans
- Your repayment period will be extended so your monthly payments may be lower
- Better control of your student loans
- Better control of your money

What are the disadvantages of consolidating your federal student loans?

- You may end up paying more interest in the long run if your repayment period is extended
- If you add your Perkins loan into the consolidation loan, you may lose some benefits, one of which is possible loan cancellation designed solely for the Perkins Loan Program.

When should you consolidate your federal student loans? You should consider consolidating your student loans at least 45 days before the end of your grace period. You can also consolidate your federal student loans when your loans are in repayment, deferment or forbearance.

How do you get the consolidation process started? Contact your lender or loan servicer for information. If your federal student loans are with Direct Loans, you can reach them online at www.direct.ed.gov. You will find the application there. There is no fee to consolidate your student loans with Direct Loans. Complete it and submit it online.

How do you know what type of federal student loans you have and the loan balances? You can find this information two ways.

1. You can contact your lender or loan servicer.
2. However, if you took out federal student loans prior to July 1, 2010 then you may have multiple lenders. If that is the case, visit the **National Student Loan Data System (NSLDS)** at www.nslds.ed.gov. You will need the Federal Student Aid PIN you created when you filled out your FAFSA to access your information. If you do not remember your 4 digit pin, go to www.pin.ed.gov to request a duplicate.

You have both private and federal student loans but can only pay one not both. What can you do? You may have graduated with private and federal student loan debt especially if you attended an expensive university. If you find yourself with little to no money to live let alone to pay student loans, take the following steps:

1. The first thing you should do is consolidate your federal student loans to lower your payments. Yes, you will have more interest to pay in the long run; however, your income right after graduating college may not be enough to cover high student loan payments. You can always increase your payments later.

2. If payments are still too high, contact your lender for both the private and federal student loans to determine what repayment plan is best for you. We went over the repayment plans offered by Federal Student Aid. Private student loan lenders may have different repayment plans. One common repayment plan they offer is an interest only plan. This means you would only be paying the interest that is accruing on the loan each month for a specified period of time. The principal balance of the student loan would remain the same however.

Tip: The **principal of a loan** is the actual dollar amount borrowed without interest and fees added. So if you are just paying the interest charge each month on your student loan, the principal balance will not decrease.

Note: If you have both private and federal student loans but cannot pay even the lowest monthly payment allowed, work on paying back your private loans first and put your federal student loans in forbearance. Often, federal student loans have longer forbearance periods and more flexible repayment terms than private student loans.

If your federal loans are with another lender, **consolidate**

your loans with Direct Loans first to take advantage of these terms. Other lenders will tell you that you have a limited number of months left or that you ran out of forbearance or deferment. Direct Loans forbearance periods are much longer.

What if you simply cannot make any payments whatsoever? Maybe, you have not found a job yet after your grace period. Contact your lenders immediately to see if you qualify for forbearance due to temporary financial hardship. If you do, you can have your student loan payment postponed (delayed) for a period of time.

Note: Temporary postponement of student loan payments is called deferment or forbearance. If your lender for your federal student loans is Direct Loans, you can ask for forbearance up to 12 months at a time. If you still need more time after the 12 month forbearance period, you must contact them again. You can reach Direct Loan Servicing Center at http://www.direct.ed.gov or 800-848-0979. If you are overseas, call 011-315-738-6634.

Now, let's discuss the different ways in which you can have your student loans forgiven, cancelled or discharged.

Forgiving, Cancelling & Discharging Student Loans

Are there other ways to pay off your student loans? Yes. There are many programs available, especially if you have federal student loans, which can assist you with paying some or all of your student loan balance. Most of these programs are based on the career path you take. For example, there are **student loan assistance programs** for primary and secondary school teachers, nurses, Peace Corp volunteers, public service employees, etc. There are also special cases where your federal **student loans can be cancelled or discharged**.

Student Loan Forgiveness

When a student loan debt is forgiven, it means you no longer have to pay that debt or remaining balance. Federal Student Aid offers one popular loan forgiveness program called the Public Service Loan Forgiveness Program.
Public Service Loan Forgiveness Program (PSLF) allows individuals who have federal Direct Loans and work for the public sector to make only 120 monthly (10 years) payments toward their student loan debt and the remaining balance will be forgiven. Meaning, after making the required 120 separate monthly payments, if there is a remaining loan balance, you will not need to pay it.

What are the qualifications for the Public Service Loan Forgiveness Program?

1. Must be employed full time in a public sector or a non-profit organization while making your student loan payments

2. Only federal student loans that have Direct Loans as lender qualify for this program. So if your **federal** student loans are with another company or lender such as American Educational Services (AES) or Sallie Mae; consolidate those loans with Direct Loans so any future payments you make can qualify

3. Each of the 120 monthly payments made must have occurred while employed in a public sector or non-profit organization. **Note:** doubling up on the payments in a month do not count as two payments.

4. The three main repayment plans that are approved for the program are the income base repayment plan, income contingent plan and the standard repayment plan.

5. Only student loan payments made on or after October 2007 will count.

6. Although it is not mandatory, it is recommended that you complete the **Employment Certification for Public Service Loan Forgiveness form**. This will help you and the U.S. Department of Education keep track of the payments you make under this program.

One of the sections of the form must be completed by an authorized person at your place of work who can certify your employment history. Once you have the form completed you can mail or fax it. The mailing address and fax number is on the form.

There is also a **Stafford Loan Forgiveness Program for Teachers**. You can learn more about this Public Service Loan Forgiveness Program at the Federal Student Aid website, www.studentaid.ed.gov

Volunteer organizations

Listed below are some of the volunteer organizations offering student loan assistance/forgiveness. You can learn more about them on their website.

- **AmeriCorps:** If you serve 12 months, you can receive up to $7,400 in stipends plus $4,725 toward your student loans. You can learn about this program at www.americorps.gov
- **Peace Corps:** As a volunteer you can apply for deferment of Stafford, Consolidation Loans, and partial cancellation of your Perkins Loans (15% for each year of service, up to 70% in total). Learn more at www.peacecorps.gov
- **Volunteers in Service to America (VISTA):** provide 1,700 hours of service and can receive $4,725. You can learn more about this program at www.americorps.gov

Do some research: If you are in the field of health, education, science, or law there may be student loan assistance programs that can help you repay your student loans. Start by talking to your academic advisor and/or your school financial aid department.

Student Loan Cancellation & Discharge

Federal student loans made under Title IV of the Higher Education Act is cancellable under certain circumstances.

Death: If you, the borrower pass away, your student loans and the parent PLUS loan your parents borrowed for you are dischargeable. This means the student loan debt will NOT be the burden of your spouse, children or parents. Your loved ones will only need to provide an original or certified death certificate to the lender or loan servicer to have the loan cancelled.

Note: If your parent borrowed a Direct Plus loan for you or someone co-signed your **private/ alternative** student loan and you pass away, your parent and the cosigner may still be responsible for the student loan.

Total & Permanent Disability (TPD): If you, the borrower, become permanently and totally disabled, send your lender or loan servicer a certified document from your doctor to confirm your condition. If you are a **veteran,** provide the documentation from the U.S. Dept. of Veteran Affairs.

Your federal student loans can also be discharged or cancelled if your school closed prior to you completing your program and in the event of falsification of your loan documents. You can learn more about forgiving and discharging your federal student loans at www.ed.gov

Defaulting on Your Student Loans

What happens if you fail to pay back your student loans? Borrowers who fail to make payments on their student loans and are not on forbearance or deferment will be considered "in default". Once your student loans go into default two key things happen.

1. You are reported to the three major credit bureaus: Experian, Trans Union and Equifax. A default of student loan is an extremely negative mark against your credit.
2. Legal action can be taken which includes having money garnished (taken out) of your paycheck and tax refunds withheld.

Many people go into default of their student loans because they do not effectively communicate with their lender or loan servicer. Additionally, they fail to plan for their repayment period. Here are some of the reasons why you may find yourself in default.

- **You do not return phone calls from lenders or loan servicer**. Return all voice messages promptly. Make sure you write down the phone number accurately and make time to call them back during the day.

- **You do not open or ignore letters from your loan servicer or lender.** Open all communication sent to you from your lender/loan servicer whether they are sent via email or snail mail. If you do not understand what you are reading, CALL your lender/loan servicer so they can explain it to you.

- **You simply avoid your student loans as if they will disappear**. The reality is that your student loans have to be repaid.
- **You overextend yourself**. If you graduate with student loan debt you should live a frugal lifestyle. This is not the time to have the latest sports car, a fancy apartment or eat out every day. Keep your monthly living expenses low enough to accommodate your student loan payments. Although it is tempting to have the newest and latest gadgets like your peers; having student loan payments will inhibit you from maintaining the pretense for long.

There is no reason why you should default on your federal or private student loans. There are several options you can take to avoid defaulting if you are having difficulty making regular payments on your student loans.

- You can ask for a lower repayment plan which can include making interest only payments for a limited time
- Get a higher paying job
- Get a part time job to supplement your income
- Ask for forbearance. Usually you can request a temporary postponement of payment due to financial hardship

Note: If you decide to continue your education and will be enrolled at least half time, you can ask your lender or loan servicer for a deferment. They may ask you for proof of enrollment.

Are you in default of your student loans? Is there anything you can do about it? Yes! Contact your lender or loan servicer and ask them what you can do to **rehabilitate** your student loans. Rehabilitating your student loans mean you have to follow certain procedures to completion before the default status can be lifted.

You may be asked to make a certain number of consecutive monthly payments. It may be 6 months or more. The key is to **pay the stated amount and pay it on time** each month. Once you have successfully met the requirements, the default status will be changed to repayment or forbearance (depending what you are approved for).

Want to hear some good news? Just because your student loans are in default it does not mean it will remain that way. The default status usually is removed from your credit report after you rehabilitate the loan.

How does defaulting on student loans affect your credit? A default of student loans keeps you from accessing credit you may need. It may also keep you from acquiring an apartment, a job, car insurance, etc. In addition, you maybe be ineligible to renew your professional license. Defaulting on your student loans creates a gridlock on your purchasing ability. Life will become very difficult financially until you take care of this issue.

How do you avoid defaulting on your student loans? As mentioned before, there should not be any reason for you to default on your student loans. There are some common sense steps you can take to avoid defaulting on your student loans.

- Remain in communication with your lender or loan servicer. For example, if you move and/or change your address, phone number & email address, let them know.
- If you are unable to make your payments, contact them immediately. Do not ignore your student loan responsibility.

What happens if you cannot get any resolution to your student loan dispute with your lender or loan servicer? There is help. The next section will discuss how.

Resolving Federal Student Loan Issues

If you are having difficulty resolving your federal student loan issues with your lender you should contact the Federal Student Aid Ombudsman office of the U.S. Dept of Education. This office created in 1998 helps borrowers of **federal** student loans resolve disputes and other problems. Before contacting the Ombudsman office make sure you understand what they can and cannot do for you.

What can the Ombudsman office do for you?

- They will act as a neutral party with an independent viewpoint to help resolve disputes

- They will accept issues relating to Direct Loans, FFEL Loans, Perkins Loan & Guaranteed Student Loans
- They will provide their service free of charge

What is the process? They will first do some research to obtain facts. Then, they will make the determination if your complaint is legitimate. If your issue is legitimate, they will work with Direct Loans on your behalf for a resolution. If your complaint is not justified, they will explain to you how they reach that conclusion.

What the Ombudsman office cannot do for you?

- They will not be an advocate or take your side. They will remain impartial.
- They do not answer general customer service questions.
- They do not handle issues regarding private/alternative student loans.
- They do not respond to inquiries regarding the Free Application for Federal Student Aid (FAFSA).

Before you contact the Ombudsman Office they want you to download the self-resolution checklist to ensure you made every attempt to resolve your issue yourself. You can learn more about them at www.ombudsman.ed.gov

Final Note

Just remember, if you borrowed student loans make every effort to repay them. This means if you have to forgo things you want now, choose to have the courage to do so. You may have to make some sacrifices in the beginning, especially right after graduation. This may include:

- Working more than one job or overtime
- Living with roommates or your parents to save money
- Forgoing purchases like a new car, large screen TV, etc.
- Bagging your own lunch to work every day instead of eating out

Also, consider working in a field that provides student loan forgiveness such as the public sector (local, state or federal government), primary or secondary education, nursing, etc. to help repay your student loans faster. Despite all the get rich schemes out there, the truth is there are no free lunches. Do not be afraid to work smart and hard.

Quick Reference Resources

To apply & check the status of your Free Application for Federal Student Aid (FAFSA) www.fafsa.ed.gov

Questions or help about your Free Application for Federal Student Aid (FAFSA): 800-433-3243

To consolidate your student loans: www.direct.ed.gov

To learn about the GI Bill: www.gibill.va.gov

To learn about different military education benefits: www.military.com

To search & apply for scholarships: www.fastweb.com and www.collegeaid.com

To complete the Master Promissory Note, Entrance & Exit Counseling: www.studentaid.com

To find the type of and balance of your federal student loans: www.nslds.ed.gov

To learn about federal student loan repayment plans: www.studentaid.ed.gov

Common Federal Student Aid Abbreviations

AL= Award Letter

AY= Academic Year

COA= Cost of Attendance

DL= Direct Loan

EFC: Expected Family Contribution

FAFSA: Free Application for Federal Student Aid

MPN: Master Promissory Note

NSLDS: The National Student Loan Data System

R2T4: Return To Title IV

SAP: Satisfactory Academic Progress

SAR: Student Aid Report

SSN: Social Security Number

Made in the USA
Monee, IL
04 November 2026

67377653R00024